A SECULAR ENCYCLICAL

*Seeing the Current State of the World
with Critical and Remedial Concern*

A SECULAR ENCYCLICAL

*Seeing the Current State of the World
with Critical and Remedial Concern*

GLENN BOYD SMITH

SUNSTONE
PRESS
SANTA FE

Sunstone books may be purchased for educational, business, or sales promotional use.
For information please write: Special Markets Department, Sunstone Press,
P.O. Box 2321, Santa Fe, New Mexico 87504-2321.
Printed on acid-free paper
∞
eBook: 978-1-61139-777-2

Library of Congress Cataloging-in-Publication Data

Names: Smith, Glenn Boyd, 1940- author.
Title: A secular encyclical : seeing the current state of the world with
   critical and remedial concern / Glenn Boyd Smith.
Description: Santa Fe : Sunstone Press, [2025] | Includes reader's guide. |
   Summary: "This work invites readers to bring attention to and change our
   current dysfunctional, destructive, divided, anxious, and fearful
   efforts into more skillful behavior"-- Provided by publisher.
Identifiers: LCCN 2025033504 | ISBN 9781632937643 (paperback) | ISBN
   9781611397772 (epub)
Subjects: LCSH: Self-efficacy. | LCGFT: Self-help publications.
Classification: LCC BF637.S38 S65 2025 | DDC 158.1--dc23/eng/20250724

LC record available at https://lccn.loc.gov/2025033504

WWW.SUNSTONEPRESS.COM
SUNSTONE PRESS / POST OFFICE BOX 2321 / SANTA FE, NM 87504-2321 /USA
(505) 988-4418

We do not need to be saved from our human condition so much as we need to learn how to live it skillfully.

—Glenn Boyd Smith

DEDICATION

The present work is dedicated to fostering true awareness, right-thinking, and right effort. If these three functions operate in concord, they will serve as our first and last refuge and as a true and wise guide in our lifelong search to find quality in human life.

If, in a mindful manner, we begin to struggle to overcome delusion, and thereby encounter understanding and insight, we are led to a correct and fruitful mode of action. This action—our behavior—is anchored in the "meaning" we have created and the values we have espoused. We are thereby led to skillful behavior—behavior that appropriately fulfills our need to achieve a state of harmony in body, mind, energy, with the natural world and all those who inhabit it along with ourselves.

If we manage to attain correct or skillful action in our daily lives, we encounter a sense of peace and happiness in the unity that we share with all. I dedicate my efforts in this regard to those who have set out on this all-important path. And in doing so, they undoubtedly now understand, with an ever-deepening inner clarity, that their commitment to pursue this path, far from being a singular mission, involves them in the dual role of helping others to take their own steps along that same route.

I dedicate and share my efforts in this initiative with all other human beings who, mindfully and with wholehearted commitment, strive to create a true meaning for themselves and a genuine sense of harmony with the natural order of things. Moreover, I aim these same efforts on my part to those others who choose to honor and give substance to the covenants of equanimity and true cooperation with others. These covenants are at the very heart of our humanity because they are the essential means to liberate us from our sorry prison to the true freedom of unity, action, and a more intensely human life. These same covenants will permit us to carry out the commitment to our life with a more vivifying sense of meaning, purpose, and peace. By the same token, they will endow us with a sure legacy to avoid many of the deep dissatisfactions and sufferings that plague us all throughout the tragic moments of our human condition.

CONTENTS

CONTENTS

INTRODUCTION

Being truly human, living well and dying well, is difficult and challenging. It is not easy to accept the responsibility that our established knowledge and values entail. This is particularly true at the present time which is characterized by great division, suffering, confusion, and fear.

Throughout its long history and cultural framework, our human race has instituted meaning and values, as well as agreements and organized structures that assist us in following its path. The truth is, however, that we are not using these aids well.

Given our current divided and crisis state, never before have we more deeply needed a reality that will turn things around and revivify us to homeostasis. That term refers to an internal state of being whereby we may maintain our essential stability or equilibrium. Achieving that balance is essential, not only for warding off our self-destruction, but to strengthen our quest to grow as human beings. The goal of this work is to attempt to aid our efforts in this quintessentially human undertaking.

The blunt truth is that we are not managing our affairs particularly well. *A Secular Encyclical* hopes to present informative and empowering suggestions and guidelines which will implicitly trigger individual motivation and behavior capable of remedying that mismanagement. It may offer, as well, certain self-recommendations to buttress remedial action that are indispensable to us, should we truly propose to improve the quality of our own life as well as the life of all human beings.

THE POVERTY YET POWER OF WORDS

Because of their intrinsic poverty, words are never quite able to express or convey their conceptual content with precision. In a surprising number of cases, our verbal expressions, even when motivated with the best of intentions and carefully thought out, fail to embody the full truth or even to approximate the reality they seek to recreate.

Our commitment and subsequent efforts to embrace the challenge of leading lives embodying true meaning and personal values in harmony with others, involve much more than words. This commitment and these efforts on our part, entail patterns of thinking and acting altruistically and compassionately as well as verbalizing these modes of existence. However, it is equally true that, at the heart of our thoughts and actions, our words—both vocal and written—constitute a fundamental means for relating to and educating one another.

Some of the words that we direct to others emerge with the confidence that they will serve as reminders that will support and strengthen the good efforts put forward by everyone. For they carry a solid commitment to pursue peace and happiness in a world which, sadly, has lost its way. But these same words, though limited in their power to conceptualize and represent, still remain harbingers of a persistent belief that we carry in our soul. And that belief, simply stated, posits that, even in this lost world of ours and even hobbled by the poverty of our words, there continue to exist situations and places where we can still openly learn, teach, and state our opinions and, through the power of our words, share that vision with all.

It is my very real hope that the words outlined in this work are read and understood beyond the barriers of any specific personal affiliation or ideology. Their aim is rather to reawaken the reader's alliance with a more universal secular contemplation. This hope is born of the possibility of a link with a broader awareness and a more profound consideration of the complexities of the human conditions. That awareness and that consideration of these human complexities must exist and function freely. That freedom is a liberation from the prejudice and compulsion of any group or belief-system which denies the relevance or legitimacy of secular human exploration and which, by claiming to hold absolutes, presumes to know the very mind of God.

The preceding discussion of the paradoxical nature of words, of their ambivalent traits of poverty and power, emphasizes an important truth for understanding how words are both essential and inadequate instruments in the dialogue between self and others. For that reason, this dual nature of the spoken and written word warrants exploration.

When oral or printed words are utilized to express a concept or reality that is essentially physical or factual, i.e. empirical, objective, or scientific, they are able to do so with a high measure of accuracy or precision. Such is the situation featured in any dialogue centering on, for example, exchanges of information that relate to objective, externally verifiable facts. In the present day, where explaining precise scientific data looms very high and very frequently in verbal usage, that function of words reigns supreme. We need only regard the pre-eminence of computer information, of Google statements, of scientific explanations, as clear proof of the kind of mission we have assigned to words in contemporary society. The word as a factual instrument wields enormous power for moderns and it is for this reason that we recognize its importance. Words carry out this task of conveying facts with enormous efficiency and accuracy and justify our belief in their potency.

But what of that other trait with which words are laden, their poverty? Here we must grasp that there is another dimension to reality for which we use words to recreate, a dimension that is every bit as vital an aspect of human reality and consciousness, but, at the same time, more elusive, more subtle, more ambiguous, and more undelineated. This is the more subjective side of reality as we experience it, the psychological dimension of being, the world which, borrowing from Plato, we may describe as "the really real reality." In fact, wisdom and practicality suggest that this "psychic" world is more central and more essential a key to our inner world than its factual counterpart.

When we seek to understand this kind of "inner" reality and how we interrelate to it or to understand it, or to explain and share it with others, we have recourse to words, just as, indeed, we must in explaining or understanding the nature of the physical world. Moreover, it is precisely when we utilize words to confront our inner world, our psychological dimension and to struggle to understand and share this reality with others, that we immediately confront the poverty of words. This is because, unlike physical reality, our inner world is essentially multivalent and infinite both in its scope and in its complexity.

And so, when we use words as tools to explore and explain finite and material reality, they show us their full evocative power and scope. However, when we employ them to capture important features of our inner realities or how we can and should interact with others, we confront the very limited power, i.e., the poverty, of our words. This sobering realization of, on the one hand, the necessity of words and, on the other, of their inherent poverty, emerges particularly when we seek to understand how we may (and should) use our two worlds, the inner world of the self, i.e., our consciousness, and the external world in which we exist, to build a true bridge between ourselves and others.

In conclusion, it is for this reason that we must understand what words, given both their power and their poverty, can and cannot do for us in our struggle to express what makes us most truly human. This will, in turn, help us grasp how necessary it is for us to persevere honestly and continuously in that struggle to understand ourselves and others and to grasp the important role words play in our life-long commitment and dedication to being truly human by rebuilding a world more oriented to human values and to others.

A SECULAR ENCYCLICAL

The term "encyclical" originates, etymologically speaking, from the Greek "en kýklios," signifying "in a circle." Since early in the Seventeenth Century, the word "encyclical" tends to have been used in English to convey a widely circulated letter or communication. The adjective "secular" in the title derives its root meaning from the Latin "saeculum" that literally signified "of an age" or "of a generation." Evolving within a Christian cultural framework, the term "saecularus" was linked to anything unrelated to religion or the supernatural, i.e., belonging to the world. "Secular" should therefore be understood not as "anti-religious" (a narrower meaning often found in a more modern interpretation) but in a broader sense of "non-religious" i.e., "of the world."

The purpose of this work entitled *A Secular Encyclical* or "Open Letter" is to present a greater measure of focused awareness and attention to various aspects of our current state of affairs, particularly to the manner in which, generally speaking, we are living and how exactly we are conducting our contemporary affairs.

It is perhaps both useful and important to point out here a fundamental but key feature of the reality in which we lead our lives. This is the fact that focusing our awareness and attention more intensely on our lives does not necessarily enable us to handle our actions more effectively in order to improve the quality of our lives. Nevertheless, it is also true that such awareness and attention can trigger self-recommendations which can help the individual to see the importance of the role played by personal responsibility in human life. Being responsible in life helps us to understand what is currently and urgently needed to change our present sorry world into a higher and more rewarding dimension of personal and collective existence.

A Secular Encyclical is a salute to those who are aware of what is required of us, if we are to exist as better human members of our present-day world. As well, it seeks to focus on the fine actions of all those who are conducting themselves in a way that brings to a proper conclusion their dual roles, as good and positive agents not only for themselves but also for others. This work is also a salute to those who recognize the need for concrete action in a broadly-based alliance with others, the aim of which is to put our affairs in order and to ward off our tendency to destroy our world. In a word, *A Secular Encyclical* is an appeal for consideration toward every single member of the human race to which we all belong.

A Secular Encyclical is thus primarily aimed at conveying the true breadth of its intent as a guide to what is essentially the highest form of human action and interaction. As well, it has two further targets. The first of these goals is to acknowledge and explore the contemporary move to what we term "secular consideration, thought rooted in worldly (non-religious or non-spiritual) criteria." Its second target is to bring into focus actions arising from our universal values, values existing independently of boundaries imposed by various ideologies, beliefs and practices which deal in absolutes and dangerously claim to exercise their own monopoly on truth and right action.

SEEING THINGS AS THEY ARE:
OUR PERPLEXED STATE

If we examine the current state of our world, we must clearly conclude that not only are we not managing our affairs well, we are really mismanaging them. Our efforts to conduct our lives effectively are largely compromised or hindered by our misguided determination to dominate one another. The principal factor and motive in our interacting with others are power-driven and that power-motive poisons and compromises our whole approach to relating to others. A true sense of responsibility to our fellow human beings and its corollary (good intent) are in large measure thereby lost or submerged. They are locked in a steadfast refusal to move beyond our personal and self-centered preferences, our revelations and affiliations. Let's call this mindset of ours what it really is: bias or prejudice or down-right self-indulgence. Whether we are aware of it or not, these interaction mechanisms imprison us in genuine crisis and we are largely powerless in our ability to overcome these internal afflictions. And the tragic result of this situation? We are bent on destroying our own lives, those of others and the world in which we are playing out the drama of human life.

Given this utterly misguided jungle of patterns motivating our soul, we are thereby compelled to live in a deeply agitated, perplexed state of being. This perplexity is further heightened and is a heavier burden to bear as it is accompanied, in our moments of introspection, by an awareness that we have the knowledge and means to solve our most complicated, most pressing and most challenging problems. This knowledge is, all too sadly alas, accompanied by our realizing that we are failing to solve those very problems.

The boundaries and resulting pressures stemming from ideology, social and economic positions, ethnic dimensions, politics and beliefs, imprison us in aggressive conflicts with one another and impose on us what we regard as an overpowering need to defend our self-centered (if not selfish) positions. We hold these positions with a curious mélange of suspicion, hatred, anger, fear and delusion. Remedial goals that could serve as the key to our prison are available, but they are anemic and come unbuttressed by the muscle necessary to trigger appropriate efforts required to reach a solution to the dilemma. Struggling fecklessly with the symptoms of our failures has become one of our chief activities rather than mustering our efforts into eliminating these failures. We are thus not only not engaged in solving the problems of how to foster what is best in our humanity and to help others to do likewise, we are increasing the intensity—and the urgency—of those problems in very unsettling and increased proportions.

We treat the events and manifestations of our sad state more as a source of entertainment or pastime than as a challenge and we compulsively explore our misguided attempts to impose mistaken goals and guidelines on one another. Faith and hope, which should be central features of our own motivations as well as those we offer others seem tragically empty and without practical effectiveness. This leads us to an even more profound emptiness in which we question whether or not there is really any valid reason left for us to justify hope for change. In such a moral wasteland as that, is it any surprise that we find ourselves on the very edge of despair?

The root cause of our tragic, divided, and dysfunctional state lies in our individual unskilled behavior, or our misguided patterns of action. However, on a more positive note, we are finally growing increasingly aware that, in our individualized as well as our collective behavior, we must move beyond the aloneness of the cellular boundaries of our affiliation mechanisms. We are also beginning to grasp that our awareness, being trapped in aloneness, is an empty insight and a sterile concept when it is not partnered with the dynamism of appropriate intent and determined effort.

Our well-being depends upon and is inextricably linked to the efforts, good will, and intellectual honesty of individuals—not only our own but that of others as well. The knowledge of the nobility of our very being and of our ultimate destination, as well as the reminders of that nobility which constantly confront us, clearly give us special power. And this is the power to create within us the confidence necessary to practice skillful thinking and motivation that will lead us to skillful action. However, it is also only too clear that we are failing to do this and one strong indication of this failure on our part is linked to persistently ignoring the teachings of so many of our great educators, guides, and motivators, past and present.

Given this sad state of failure that we must acknowledge, what is the challenge that it presents to us? It is nothing less than our duty and indeed our obligation to turn things around radically. That duty and obligation entail influencing and triggering modes of behavior within ourselves that will fulfill both our own individual needs and objectives and those same needs and objectives which we share with our fellow human beings. Expressed in essence, that challenge is simply "learning how to live with what we are and who we are."

We are living in days of deep darkness and grave crises. Yet our present age is, all things considered, also a time of great opportunity. Our future will be determined, to a very marked extent, by our openness and positive bias to teach, to learn, and to unlearn—to practice skillful behavior and to cease clinging to the emotionally laden, primitive, and sterile conduct of our past.

Never before have we possessed the abundant knowledge and broad access to human and natural resources that permit us to achieve the widely shared aspiration—indeed the dream—to find the path leading us to peaceful coexistence, harmony, equanimity and justice. Individual change in behavior, once it is raised to the level of collective action, is our challenge and the basis of our hope for change—a change to halt the destruction we seem bent on pursuing—and thereby to initiate and sustain remedial and true human development.

The term "development" used here warrants some measure of exploration for two reasons. Firstly, it is a subtle, multifaceted, all-encompassing, concept and, secondly, it plays a vital role in the evolution of a human person from being merely potentially human to being actual or fully human. Broadly speaking, "development" involves our growth whereby we mature as individual beings existing and functioning naturally and simultaneously on several different yet interconnected levels: the material, the intellectual, the moral, the cultural, the social, and the spiritual. Our inchoate nature begins in pure potentiality, marked primarily and essentially only as the power to be infinitely richer and more fulsome than our genesis. In fact, at our genesis moment, we are as much creatures of the future as we are of the present. The root meaning of "future" carries the key to understanding what we really mean by "development." If we explore the Latin origins of the term "futurus" we find that it is the future participle of the verb "to be" (esse) and translates into English not as "to be" but rather as "to be about to be." So when we describe ourselves not only as creatures "of the present" but also as creatures "of the future" we are really stating that not only we are "what we *are*" but we are also what we are *going to be*."

So what exactly does our "development" involve? First of all, "development" brings into focus the importance of "otherness." By that we mean we cannot truly understand our own identity unless we see that our sense-of-self is inextricably linked to the self-of-the-other. This, in turn, brings into focus that we must instinctively and spontaneously assign to others the same importance that we naturally assign to ourselves...no more but no less.

Development also entails a deepening sense of the fact that our individuality, our sense of being unique, in no way conflicts with what links all of us together as human beings. In other words, being independent should not mean being separated and certainly not being isolated. Development thus signifies not only growing but growing together. It means, when all is said and done, taking a more complete possession of our individual existence by taking a more complete possession of our communal existence.

Our approach to this sort of fundamental behavioral change must, of course, include our awareness and understanding that we will succeed in that endeavor only if we make better and wiser use of the many organized structures we have succeeded in creating. That is undoubtedly not only the best—perhaps the unique—means for us to give reality to truly worthwhile solutions of our pressing problems. In our dealings with others and as individuals striving to cultivate true humanism, we must strive to make our human interrelationships function on the collective level. If we do this successfully this collective behavior will thereby strengthen our influence in dealing with others and, what is even more important, will enhance and enrich both their lives and our own. The principles and mechanisms that come into play in human interrelatedness and interdependence are clearly understood and acknowledged. Therefore, it is to the wise and consistent application and use of these principles in our daily lives and in our links to those around us that we must now allot much more attention.

OUR NEED FOR GLOBAL SECULAR ACTION

Our predispositions of thought and action, when they function within the boundaries of our belief systems, have always exercised a very potent influence on human thought, development, and positive action. It is equally clear that these biases have also often prevented our local and global collaboration in matters of unity and in our ability to further equanimity and social and cultural development. These belief boundaries have also contributed to the prevention of authentic international covenants and practical problem-solving protocols. These long-standing practices of our belief systems continue to teach and dictate that our spirituality is something apart from the secular. By marginalizing secular values these traditional and long-standing belief systems continue to exercise a markedly negative influence on human behavior and development.

It is important to acknowledge the lingering misconception that one cannot hold individual beliefs while working for and with others within a system using universal values and procedures. This persistent error represents one of the major barriers to our ability to develop a sense of communality. The question that naturally and inevitably arises is exactly how this ill-perceived barrier between my beliefs and my commitment to others can be overcome in order to show that appropriately structured communal covenants and individual values need not alienate our helping others. This, in turn, will aid us in rethinking our misguided conviction that individual beliefs are opposed to communal cooperation. Our tendency to feel that, if we cannot impose our own values on others, then we can't interrelate with them. Such a mindset is particularly destructive of a communal spirit because it assumes that I have no duty to help others unless they accept that my values are absolute and must be theirs as well.

In spite of our great divisions and our penchant to cling instinctively to primitive practices, there is much developing in our awareness nowadays to give us solid reason for great hope and cautious optimism. In the question of control and maintenance of traditions, for example, we are taking steps to free ourselves from the tyranny of the past. Specifically, our more modern sense of awareness is moving us, gradually but steadily, towards acknowledging that we are first human beings in a world of other human beings. In doing so, we are taking real steps to see that one of our most urgent needs is to use universal secular intent and action in understanding ourselves and others and in our relationships with fellow human beings. We are thus escaping from the thralls of primitive thought, of controlling action and the bondage of absolutes. In many cases, we are also moving away from corrupt and misguided moral, social, and cultural management, as well as aggressive control imposed upon us by large organizations and institutions.

So, despite the fact that our journey is far from its ultimate goal of finding true enlightenment and of existing as better, more compassionate and more "human" beings, it is still safe to say that the world is advancing. We see this as real, though limited, progress in thought, purpose, and action sustained by a commonly-held system of values. This progress gives stronger meaning and purpose to our unity of intent by furnishing practical plans to continue to improve the conditions that promote equanimity and quality of life. This movement, still fragile and still challenged by our old ways of thinking and acting, needs to be protected and strengthened in order to overcome and eliminate the threatening and potentially harmful effects we ourselves have also created.

WHO WE ARE AND WHAT WE KNOW

We are born into this world as individuals, not knowing with any certainty why we are here or even if that "why" has an answer. The heart of what we may term "the human dilemma" is simple but stark and is a two-sided coin. On the face is the unsettling realization that, even though we know life is real and compelling, can we reasonably believe we will ever find a way to live happily and well, to create a "modus bene vivendi?" The reverse side of this human dilemma tells us that, although we are uncertain of what kind of a deal fate may deign to give us; we have no choice but to adapt to life. Moreover, we wonder where much of our strength and weakness comes from and where our character, our personality and our ability to develop our traits have their origin. Moreover, we are often driven to wrestle with a deeper, more elusive question: after all is said and done, has our individual predisposition to life been designed and foisted on us for any purpose at all? In other words, is life something real or just an unfathomable chance or, worse still, a cruel and tragic joke?

Human existence may well be much less complex and more easily explained and understood than, historically speaking, we have been led to believe. We are alone. Many of the supernatural realities, i.e., the gods and demons, whom we have so meticulously created over countless ages, now hold only delusional power over us. The equation of a human species sustained, explained, and justified only by referring its origins to some extra-terrestrial dimension has been largely shelved, though it has taken quite a lengthy time-span to find that shelf!

Instead, we have metamorphosed into a biological species that has managed to adapt itself to a world of "others." Our developed awareness, problem-solving ability, and the creation of meaning and intent (free will) have brought us to the point where, in egregious audacity, we deem ourselves to be unique in the world. We regard our greatest accomplishments, whether cultural, social, scientific or technological, as unquestioned proof that we are right in assigning ourselves to this lofty and unique locus in the cosmos. However, if we are also brutally honest and realistic with ourselves, we will see that our great achievements may also betray a darker side to our assumed "superiority." Such an insight may well make us admit that what, in our vanity, we see as our grandest accomplishments in our world and in ourselves are in fact too often very self-defeating and destructive. In other words, many of us now sense that our so-called triumphs have created deep divisions in how we conduct ourselves and how we relate to others.

More and more of us may in fact have begun to question the meaning and worth of what we have created. This shadow of doubt is particularly evident in how randomly we interact with others. This randomness is evident in how we use our covenants, spoken, legislated, or implied, and how remiss we are in taking remedial action against the crises that our moral laziness creates in a divided state. The result of this unsettling state of affairs is that we currently live in an unsatisfactory and ignorant communal realm under a tragic cloud of anguish and crisis.

We inhabit a world, therefore, that we have developed and exist as beings of our own making. So, if our environment and our present state of nature are unsatisfactory—and they surely are on both counts—we really have no one to blame but ourselves. How and whether we continue with that kind of framework or attempt to alter it is up to us and will be determined by the action we now take at this time of crisis. We are who we are because of our behavior, by the choices we have made and not simply because we live within the forces of many natural processes.

Our species has evolved and developed awareness, knowledge and free will. These rational faculties give us great power both to build and destroy. Our repertory of intellectual and moral skills also carries the ability to envisage the reality we call change and to bring it to fruition by the conscious and determined aim of establishing (or restoring) equilibrium to the world we inhabit.

Our cultural, social, and philosophical history is essentially an account of how we have built our knowledge of how we relate to and exploit our human nature and its inherent powers as well as how we can and should interrelate with fellow humans. This corpus of intellectual, social, and scientific knowledge of ourselves and our world, which we have garnered over the centuries, thanks to a host of great teachers, has brought us to greatness by providing us with the wherewithal to transform our nature's potentiality into actuality. We must continue with vigor and confidence to engage in this very significant exploration of who we are and the actualization of what we can be.

Wisdom also dictates that we should conduct the exploration and actualization of self, society, and others within a mindset characterized by maximum awareness. This awareness will keep a central truth in focus: in spite of the barriers and divisions which dog our interaction with others, as a cultural presence, we are capable, whether as individuals or as a community, to come up with answers and solutions to our common problems. These protocols will engender wisdom, equilibrium, and harmony in our sorry state. That same profound awareness will affirm that we can bring harmony and order as well to our never-ending journey of development and progress. If we ever hope to achieve this elusive but all-important goal, we must act in a context of unity. And that context of unity consists of our actions being universal and secular. In other words, our contact and relationship with others must be clearly and strongly characterized by a true sense of collectivity and otherness anchored not in any immaterial dimension but squarely in this world.

What have we already accomplished? Much! We can now recognize an essential truth: what lies at the heart of what we term our "fundamental human condition" and what we need to do to find the knowledge, courage, and commitment to live a meaningful life. Paradoxically, we are also painfully aware of the existence of this essential truth because of our failures and mistakes. This underlines the Cartesian insight that error, when recognized and acknowledged, can teach us as much (if not more) about ourselves and reality than truth. Our misguided actions, arising from our motives and our behavior, we now see have been both skillful and unskillful. That is progress of a sort! Nevertheless, we certainly are still not out of the woods in this regard! The unskillful behavior which we sometimes still cling to and which prevents progress, mistakenly and tragically lives on too frequently in the extreme and still threatens to compromise our existence. This ubiquitous risk must be recognized, addressed, and confronted. If that occurs, we will only then succeed in bringing ourselves from our current divided and destructive state back to the path of secular salvation. In other words, we must increase our awareness of the need to change our ancient mindset of unsecular domination and control to one solidly anchored to world-centered collaboration and effective action.

HOW WE FIND MEANING AND PURPOSE

We live our lives within the framework of actions involving many constantly changing processes. As for the answers to the deeper questions of what meaning and purpose does our existence have, the answers are somehow always tentative and elusive. We find these responses sometimes through mindful reflection and consideration, sometimes through superficial and heedless acceptance of our thoughts, and sometimes through our interactions with one another and with the world around us.

The first focus of awareness is the self, which then leads us to find meaning in our awareness of others, usually through their expressions, beginning with the first glimpse of a parent's face. From that initial awareness experience, we continue our exploration and begin to interact with others. By expanding these interactions, we are gradually able to create a sense of what "otherness" truly means. This is what finding out what meaning really means.

In that primary and embryonic awareness, we instinctively recognize and experience different aspects of ourselves as the vehicle whereby we individuate, study, and explain ourselves in our attempt to improve the quality of our lives. First, we endeavor to avoid suffering. Then we try to enhance the quality of life, either our own or the life we share with others, by creating informal or formal covenants. These covenants we activate and implement through negotiated agreements and through control with laws, which we establish within these agreements.

In the initial stages of our evolution, we evolved in relatively isolated small groups. In time, through systematic encounters with other groups, we experienced the benefits of assertive and collaborative action. We also learned of the benefit of aggressive action, which we needed to protect, defend, and impose our particular values and customs on one another. Through these growing instances of social interaction and with the world we shared, our self-knowledge grew. We thereby found increased meaning and understanding not only of our own self and the other's self, but we also acquired an important insight: the interrelationship of selves—mine and theirs—yields per se a valuable and useful insight and deepens our understanding of the meaning of "the other."

In the beginning, through the awareness that came to us when we sensed that we are interrelated with all and yet alone, independent, and unique, we also began to grow aware of how we must function. We found a way to live. In that vague, semi-instinctive, semi-intuitive, initial awareness of our individual and collective aloneness, we also found meaning and value in our integration with one another and with the world beyond our individual selves. Now, in this modern age, we have the opportunity to apply the knowledge we found through our long efforts to evolve and adapt. So we are no longer compelled to cling to those ancient tactics and mindsets that now serve more to divide us than to integrate. Instead, we must learn to use what we know will bring authentic results in our pursuit of development, protection, and improvement of our lives.

We live our lives as both individuals and members of collectives as well as integrated elements of our environment. In our efforts to decide how best to conduct ourselves we must never forget that this covenant comprises not only ourselves, but also others as well as the world that provides the locus for that covenant. Nor can we permit ourselves to forget or ignore that we also function within the limitations of our nature and our individual traits. However, let us also be mindful that we possess moral freedom to choose the way we behave. Our awareness of this self-knowledge comes with time, experience, and change. That is because we decide our actions, based upon what we discover and what we are taught, as well as what has been revealed to us by our experiences and the input and influence of our affiliations.

How we conduct ourselves within the known body of our resources, meaning, values, skills, principles, covenants, and structures, can bring us to the celebration of a life richer and more truly human than would otherwise be the case. Such a lifestyle has a much better chance of bringing us to a heightened sense of happiness and serenity rather than to a state of confusion, anguish, and great suffering. It is for this reason that skillful behavior must always be our primary concern and goal. And what exactly does that expression mean? Simply put, skillful behavior is nothing more than integrating into our personal actions and our interactions with others all the hard-won awareness of who we really are, of who they really are and therefore of how we should interact with them. Conversely, "unskillful behavior" enters the picture when that hard-won awareness and sensitivity to others are absent. Therefore, as long as we have a consistent and strong commitment to true awareness in our lives, we will have a very good chance to protect ourselves and our world from the kind of chaos and terrible crises we now experience. Even more to the point, we will thereby create an action framework leading to beneficial ongoing planning, problem-solving, and optimal functioning.

SKILLFUL BEHAVIOR

The skillful aspect of skillful behavior, as referred to here, involves the wisdom and appropriateness of assessing and planning our actions, which must occur prior to our actually carrying out these actions. Our behavior is simply executing these actions. This behavior becomes skillful if it arises from our appropriate mindful attention to the issues and duties operating in our personal lives and in whatever affiliation we find ourselves engaged. Stated directly, skillful behavior is "doing the right thing." It is behavior based on and guided by the universal principles, mores, and ethics that we as humans have established and which serve our own legitimate needs and the needs of others. It is behavior that enhances the quality of life and in doing so, thereby produces goodwill, unity, happiness, and peace. It is our conduct. It is imposing effective control over our fundamental tendencies of greed, self-centeredness, anger, and delusion. It is replacing those weaknesses with generosity, respect, kindness, and wisdom. It is the creative and practical application of our developed values. It is the type of behavior that we bring to bear on our collective action and to our organized management of local and global affairs. It is behavior that demonstrates acceptance of our responsibility for our own well-being and the well-being of others. It is behavior that does no harm and that is effective. It is our refuge and our strength and the clearest indication that we are willing and able to allow what is truly human in our nature to take the lead among the many possible motives which move us to action.

If we seek to identify why we have been brought to our present state of crisis at all levels of society, we find it in our ubiquitous failure to accept our quintessential responsibilities as human beings and to "do what is right." It is our failure to practice skillful behavior, and to eliminate unskillful behavior—our selfishness, lack of discipline, greed, anger, delusion, ignorance, and the hurtful and detrimental action arising from ill-will.

What is necessary if we are truly committed to live under the guidance of meaning that we have established and implemented within ourselves as the fundamental feature of the human condition? It quite simply demands nothing less of us than to create and manage our own individual affairs and those of others within the rationally considered framework of time, place, and thought.

In order to live, both individually and collectively as human beings in a relatively peaceful and constantly developing state, we must acknowledge the fundamental realities of need, dissatisfaction, and ignorance in which we hold our existence. If we manage to keep those essential realities alive in our minds, this will lead us to see the corollary, namely that we need to control our greed, anger, and delusions. We must constantly engage in establishing a definition—tentative and unguaranteed though it may be—of what and who we are. We must also establish value systems, identify our true human needs, and incorporate resulting protocols, once established, into practical procedures of discipline and formally established, binding agreements.

Without such appropriate practical structures, which allow for development and control, with provision for evaluation and growth, we are marooned in an unworkable and childish stage of sentience. In such an inchoate framework, we would be unable to enjoy the noble, bountiful, and meaningful existence that we had hoped to achieve. We would be alienated from ourselves, from one another, and from our world that is meant to function as our home, and worst of all, we would be quite unable to tackle our current decline as human beings and work toward obviating our tragic state of crisis.

ACTION IN OUR CURRENT DIVIDED STATE

Although our present situation indeed leaves much to be desired, we still have both the knowledge and the enabling structures within our organizations to allow us to continue to develop. With these elements at our disposal, we have the capability, indeed the power, to raise ourselves from our current state of great suffering and potential destruction to something much more promising and enriching. The problem is that: we are not implementing or adopting our knowledge or these enabling structures to tackle the tragic and major difficulties in which we presently find ourselves and our world hopelessly mired. More than that is our consistent and prolonged failure to develop or reform our systems of consultation and dialogue. These systems are intended to bring us beyond the wasteland of feckless and ill-aimed debate, aggressive dialogue, and the sterile mentality of seeing our differences as hostile "sides" to be eliminated rather than as possibly new perspectives to enrich and unify us.

We live frozen in private and isolated domains and in our solitary and divided states we create even more crises and destruction that serve only to heighten that isolation. We are no longer capable of solving problems honestly or as integrated persons who enjoy a meaningful link with others or with the world as our shared environment. In our refusal to accept in practice the universal value of unity of intent and communal action, we are unable to free ourselves from the many crises that clearly point to death or destruction. Tragically, we mistake unity for sameness and deny the reality of the clear possibility that unity exists in diversity and in different outlooks and practices.

We are misusing our diversity to create division instead of harmony and we continue to cling to outdated aggressive practices whenever we seek to resolve problems and differences. Too often we still resort to armed conflict in seeking to resolve our confrontations with others and in our protocols for condemning others at all levels. By resorting too easily and too frequently to this way of confronting differences, we cannot yet seem to activate our problem-solving skills when facing the crises that now pressure us into anguish and despair.

We have been brought to our current unsatisfactory and tragic state of affairs by many factors. Chief among them is our very antisocial and hostile manner of behaving which arises from divisions in boundaries created by our barriers of ideology, creed, race, religion, and power groups. Instead of engaging in these negative and alienating modes of conduct, the positive pressure and influence of enlightened affiliation and bridge-building would undoubtedly encourage and sustain good action. The above barriers can also engender an unhealthy imbalance in our intellectual and emotional functioning, which in turn, can readily lead to dishonesty, unwitting errors in thought, and poor decision-making. The result of this mental and moral disarray is simple: we fail to grasp and therefore to acknowledge in our daily lives and practice that, as members of the human race, we are profoundly interrelated and truly interdependent. That being the case, it follows that every single one of us is equally responsible for all the human activity, social, political, cultural, and moral, which arises in our world.

Because of our current state of ultra-dividedness and also because of the escalation of populism as a contemporary socio-political phenomenon, we tend to accept only very limited responsibility for our failure in interrelated conduct. We take action primarily within the limiting barriers of our personal ideological, racial, religious, societal, political beliefs, or whatever other affiliation we happen to espouse. Our actions engendered in this state prevent development and simply condemn us to play out patterns of conduct towards others that are and have proved themselves to be sterile, ineffective, and counter-productive. To those on whom we impose this mode of conduct, we cause not only anger, fear, competition, hatred, and indifference, but we also contribute to our own misguided mental activity and utilize false principles. To make matters worse, this sad state of misdirected mental activity too often leads us to indulge in drugs that cause illness and alter our patterns of thinking and our ability to plan our conduct wisely and compassionately. We have thus lost our ability to control violence and corruption in our social dealings with others and in safeguarding our common environment. Not only that, we increase the violation of the covenants, traditions, and laws that we have developed over centuries in order to raise the quality of life for ourselves and for those we call our colleagues.

In many cases, we also seem to have lost confidence in our governing structures. These we have struggled mightily and for so long to establish, being convinced of their proven potential to reform our weaknesses and to develop our more promising human qualities. Our futile efforts to resolve our differences by marching and venting our anger verbally in street demonstrations do little to cure our problems and, on the contrary, simply draw more attention and awareness to our poor and divisive conduct.

Law and order still function as an important safeguard and refuge in democratic nations. However, we have problems implementing socio-political management and control that are essential adjuncts to law enforcement. This weakening of law-and-order stems from our failure to understand clearly the role we can and must play to strengthen that essential feature of the modern world. That role includes using skillful behavior, avoiding or minimalizing unskillful behavior, and eliminating exaggerated leniency in the administration of our laws.

The single most important feature that our world should seek to foster if it hopes to be able to describe itself as truly good and honest is justice. Tragically, it is justice that has largely lost its preeminent place and function in our societies and has been reduced to a dangerously minor and marginal role in our world-view and in our political and social actions. Our understandably primeval and fundamentalist view of the human condition that prevailed early on in various regional histories, had led us to accept, among other beliefs, which in problem-solving might is right. Our early social experiences in daily life seemed to prove to us that aggressive action is a good, practical way to deal with challenge and competition, or to advance, safeguard, and preserve our personal or collective needs, preferences, and ideologies. Aggressive actions also became our refuge and reaction mechanism when we met with failure in our efforts to get what we wanted.

In the beginning, this conviction that aggressive action was "the best way to go" may well have been regarded as a necessary or at least a workable stance. However, even though we have learned better, this key feature of our primitive mindset tragically remains very much with us. It has stubbornly remained rooted not only in the attitude of far too many of us, but also in the mechanisms for organized action at all levels of society. What was once our ostensible refuge is now our persistent nemesis.

This mindset—this clinging to aggression as a modus operandi, hinders our full acceptance and practice of an important universal principle. This principle states that any constructive action, any progress, or any positive development that we propose as a possible route to follow, will come about only by building on the positive rather than by embracing the negative. For example, if we see no positive value in constructive criticism, we will almost certainly mishandle our reaction to it by attacking the critic with an aggressive mindset and, in doing so, we exacerbate the situation and miss the most effective way to solve the problem in question. In denigrating constructive criticism by regarding it as dangerous and ill-intentioned, we only create more anger, disharmony, conflict, and discord, as well as an unnecessarily competitive attitude in our actions and our relationships with others.

If we propose to "turn over a new leaf" in our personal and social conduct, we should engage in action that we know to be skillful, in order to create the positive and forward-moving outcome we seek. At the same time, we must "unlearn" or provide for control of our emotionally laden aggressive attitudes. This need is clearly evident for the proper and smooth functioning of both our political and social systems and particularly in the implantation of consultation processes.

We have largely lost control over violence and corruption in modern society and one consequence of this loss is our contributing to the violation of many of the fine covenants and laws we have striven to develop over centuries. Any socio-political control that has managed to survive is now largely ineffectual because of continued and growing compromise, accommodation, and leniency.

Despite this dangerous tendency on our part to let these negative policies and attitudes prevail in our present world, we have still managed to establish, organize, and develop at various levels a bevy of systems to help us manage our affairs with integrity and justice. These management protocols are best anchored in core, universally recognized and accepted values, such as justice, truthfulness, equanimity, courage, benevolence, and conscientiousness.

Another aspect of our socio-political affairs that we are not managing very well is how we interact with our organization-governing structures and this is because of our failure to act with skillful behavior. Our divisional thinking and misdirected partisan behavior, our clinging to an aggressive lifestyle, our tendency to leniency, and our mistaken idea of self-determination, all prevent us from controlling our behavior towards ourselves and others wisely and effectively. This, in turn, compromises the proper functioning of our organized collective management of human affairs in democratic countries. In addition, it should be pointed out, as well, that, whereas we can detect the wrong ways we interact with virtually all our social, cultural, and political institutions, our failures in the way we regard and interact with our government structures are particularly obvious. Too often, we perceive government as an opponent rather than as a partner. Our misguided negativity and aggressive behavior toward government institutions eliminate or seriously erode our spirit of political cooperation. It is this absence of a positive pro-government esprit in our political ethos that lies at the root of our inability to respond appropriately to the vital needs we observe in our fellow political constituents. When our countrymen urgently voice a political problem they wish to have alleviated, instead of addressing our efforts to move government to tackle that issue, we feel there is nothing we can do to get our elected political leaders to help our fellow citizens. Worse still, we do not care and so cannot be bothered to take up their cause.

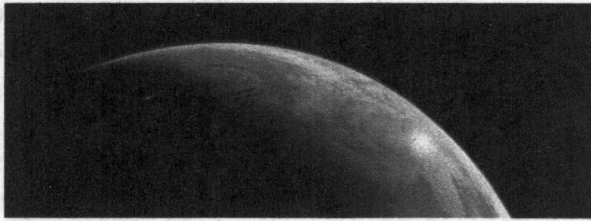

CREATING A VISION OF CHANGE

The more human beings succeed in "developing" (as that term is understood in this work) the more they grow successful in practicing skillful behavior in dealing with personal covenants and interacting with whatever group or organized collective they find themselves linked to. This ongoing need to evaluate and change our behavior in dealing with others or with the world we all call "home" has been with us virtually throughout human history. It has made itself known in different cultural contexts, using different words and for different reasons and has been eloquently expressed and promoted by humanity's greatest and wisest voices as well as by our lowliest teachers. It is with greater urgency today that the message, which this need carries, must be heeded, in the context of our ever-shrinking world of interrelatedness and interdependence. In addition, it must be incorporated in our thinking as one of our primary motives for action and indeed as a central principle of our moral systems. We simply will not survive, even in a developmental state, if we do not heed, promote, and adhere to this clarion call aimed at embracing evaluation and change of behavior.

Our behavior in how we live, is largely floundering if not completely out of control and our numerous organizations, those structures within which we practice our social covenants, have begun to deteriorate more than they are developing. This is because of the unskillful behavior we too often regularly incorporate into our actions. Much of this erosion in our socio-political and cultural organizations comes from the random and uncontrolled action of ill will. Within our organizations, specifically our political and legislative and judicial bodies, we certainly have all the necessary means and personnel to permit continued socio-political growth and development and for the improvement of the quality of life. Furthermore, we have everything we need to be able to control our destructive unskillful behavior. However, while these organizations or structures exist at the personal, local, or national level, the means whereby they could foster proper socio-political growth and development do not exist as they lack sufficient binding powers or jurisdiction at a global or international level. Codified and legally binding legislation, aimed at serving humanity and teaching us to control misguided human behavior, do not exist as world-wide legal realities and function only in theory or as fragmented legal realities. Various organized efforts in these areas do in fact exist. Too many of them operate only within the barriers of covenants primarily created from motives promoting self-preservation, protection, conquest, control, or competition. In many instances, these motives rise from deeply rooted sentiments of anger, greed, and ignorance, sentiments that, sadly, have been—and still are—a key part of our fundamental conditioned behavior.

Unless and until we have comprehensive planning to create binding global recognition and covenants with real teeth, which would apply to all aspects of individual and collective health and welfare, as alluded to in the 1948 Universal Declaration of Human Rights, we will not make real progress in what we term the "authentic development" of our human potential.

Without binding legislation at a global, international level, we are unable to practice fundamental action or exercise our responsibilities arising from our dual role as human beings. On the broadest international scale, we need the means to achieve the same sort of solid legal guides to socio-political interaction and conduct that individual nations have. That is binding legislation promulgated through democratic decision-making and negotiated covenant.

When all is said and done, we will not have even commenced to accept our responsibility for the requirements and demands of our social and cultural networks and the political structures that we have created unless we meet those requirements and demands. Nor will we have truly set about tackling the onerous task of recuperating from past blindness and activating the ongoing development of quality of life at every level and for every person on this planet until we compel each other to put the word to the deed and transform love and inner conviction into external action.

WHAT NEEDS TO HAPPEN

We have a great need to bring rational management to our conceptual analyses, to our decisions, and to our daily affairs. If we do so, this will bring balance to the kind of life that we should try to live. And that is a life framed by deep harmony with reality in general, with our world, with our own existence, and with that of our colleagues sharing that same world.

It should be clearly pointed out, in practical yet urgent terms, that never before have we as human beings, found ourselves in so great a need of a whole spectrum of wise, well-thought-out activities. Among these, we would include an empowering awareness, the ability, and willingness to reflect or meditate and the pursuit of educative action. These needs stem simply from the fact that, as conscious and moral persons, we are individuals who accept responsibility for what we are and what we do and who practice awareness and meaning in the individual and collective lives that we as humans have brought into existence.

Developed persons, practicing skillful behavior both as individuals and members of the collective within which they may find themselves—from partnership and family to international organized structures, will bring the needed change which we reckon is necessary not only for progress but for survival. Our law-making, governance, and problem-solving institutions will remain dysfunctional and incompetent without their members' practicing skillful assessment, planning, and actions aimed at dealing with crises and problems. As well, these citizens require generally speaking, the commitment and willingness to employ progressive and rational management in their individual and communal affairs.

The misuse of the individual's personal power is most frequently the cause of both one's personal problems and the crises one finds in one's interaction with others and with socio-political structures. It is equally true that this same personal power if wisely and properly used, can steer one away from the deluded path of destruction that one may be currently following. Those individuals who have great personal or delegated legislative power as leaders and lawmakers are vested with an extraordinary responsibility in this regard. There is no greater instance of harmful and divisive behavior than the conduct of politicians when they act unskillfully—selfishly, immorally, or unwisely, by not serving the legitimate needs of their constituents.

Even worse, when they act in that way, politicians or governors function as barriers to development. In fact, one of the reasons we and our world are in such tragic and widespread difficulty is that global leaders have too often failed to understand their true role as political captains. That true role, simply put, consists of exercising their duty to provide authentic dual role action (legislative and executive). It involves formulating and enacting clear, firm guidelines and binding covenants for the individuals and groups under their jurisdiction to follow. As well as their failure to fulfill the above positive side of their mission as politicians, these leaders too often inadvertently or passively support the many tyrants who reject justice and thereby do great damage to the collective welfare. In accepting or condoning tyranny, our political leaders act without any commitment to justice and legitimate political control and thus jeopardize our very existence. In some cases, this may take them as far as threatening nuclear action to elicit citizen compliance. This state of governmental institutions clearly shows the failure of our political leaders to assess, plan, and manage our affairs within the framework of a rational, just, and morally sensitive ethos and mindset.

Our body of knowledge of the most effective and truly human means to conduct ourselves both as rational individuals and as members of human society emerges from an endless amalgam of extraordinary teachers, leaders, and inspirers. Some of these educators filled different roles and wore a variety of hats. Some explicitly labelled themselves teachers, leaders, clerics, shamans, gurus, advisors, parents, brothers, and sisters, while others bore no honorific. Those leaders, past and present among us, who have achieved great knowledge and have used that knowledge to evolve true insight and a state of goodwill, speak to us, not as saviors, but as enablers and motivators of skillful behavior. The teaching of our educators carries with it an appeal to heed duty and practice compassion for others, as do the words in which their doctrines are expressed. The power of their appeal as teachers and guides, while intended for humanity in its universality, is directed to all of us as individuals, to other educators, as well as to law-makers at every level of society.

Our divided states, being too often hopelessly on the defensive, prevent us from readily accepting the key premise that individual behavior, enacted without reference to others, is our greatest problem and that incorporating "otherness" into our moral fabric must be the starting position in our striving to solve the world's problems. We often tend to turn our attention prematurely and blindly to our organizations and groups, particularly governments. We do so particularly when we are formulating the plans we should follow and the efforts we should make, in the management of our own affairs, but also when we assume the role of decision-makers in interacting with fellow persons.

While it is true that our organized structures and institutions are where socio-political planning and action are conceived and produced, within these groups very often it is individuals, not organizations who make decisions. When individuals, who are engaged in controlling our affairs and in legislating how we are expected and permitted to live, act with ill-will or with unskillful behavior, we invariably suffer. These political overseers, to the extent that they are able to legislate public actions, have the power to bring us to great suffering or to peace and unity. The remedial quality of the decisions made in our world beset with current great need and crises is thus largely dependent upon the measure of skillful behavior possessed and exercised by those decision-makers. Though we all, in a limited measure make decisions affecting others' lives, this power is much greater in the case of those with political or governmental power to manage our affairs and to instigate and support, for example, urgently needed education programs on how we all should live.

PERSONAL CONDUCT
AND WORLDWIDE PROBLEMS

Let us consider the increase in the number of individuals whom we can identify as "persons of good will." Essentially, such persons practice dual-role skillful behavior, at whatever is their level of constituency. Within their given group or organization, they may or may not be directly involved in creating mandates with appropriate binding legislation and control. Let us consider these individuals, acting with appropriate assertive behavior, from the perspective of how they may have a role to play in confronting some of the world's present problems. Such persons of good will are a very positive and beneficial social presence for us all as they believe they exist primarily to apply wise and enlightened problem-solving dynamics and their dual-role skillful behavior to their fellow citizens. As such, they are undoubtedly able to help resolve some of the world's significant problematic issues. The problem areas in the modern world within which these persons of good will play a key and beneficial role are intimidatingly numerous and include the following : The Mental Health Crisis, Drug Use, World Poverty, Climate Change, Mass Migration, Displaced Persons Crisis, Current and Future Pandemics, Health Care, Disability Rights, Corruption, Authoritarianism, LGBTQ Issues, Reproductive Justice, Children's Rights, Gender Equality, Cybersecurity, Disinformation, Freedom of the Press, Debt Crisis, Global Cooperation, Local and Global Conflict, and the Increase in Violent Crime.

At the center of every one of these critical issues is an individual suffering, perhaps in great agony, who may die prematurely and tragically abandoned. At the heart of each of these worldwide crises, too, and playing therein an important role, whether positive or negative, is the reality of our human behavior, skillful or unskillful. If we function there as an agent of unskillful behavior, we must accept our failure in exacerbating the tragedy. This failure includes our responsibility for worsening these world problematic issues that feed the miasma of destruction, harm, and suffering at the heart of the human condition. Our tragedy here is, therefore, our failure to lead lives guided by meaning, rationally formulated moral values, and incorporating the kind of truly human actions that we would otherwise perform as agents of positive change, if only we were consistently motivated by the qualities we associate with "persons of good will."

LIVING OUR MEANING AND VALUES—OUR HOPE

The kind of action we need to perform in order to release us from whatever crisis or problem in which we may be enmeshed, either as individuals or collectives, must come from a realization and acceptance of our own responsibility in creating that problem. This responsibility will compel us, as individuals or members of a collective, to avail ourselves of whatever resources are at hand and to act skillfully in meeting our needs and the needs of others. The ultimate goal of our efforts to solve our particular problem goes beyond our personal crisis and becomes much greater in scope. It is no less than attempting to maintain or improving the quality of life, not just our own but that of others. In this way, what seems on the surface to be "little me" solving my own little difficulty gives me the chance to act courageously and selflessly; to practice true meaning and to acknowledge the noble value of the personal covenant I owe to others as a good human being.

It is only in accepting who we are and then in proceeding to demonstrate through our actions the positive and transformative qualities of who we are that we have any real hope to resolve the difficulties we have created for ourselves and our world. This repossession of our nature will then enrich us with hope and confidence. That hope and confidence become not only the means to halt what may well be our impending destruction but also to put us back on the path to the peaceful existence that humanity has so long desired. This radical shift in our attitudes and actions will bring us back to a delicate but all-important balance between living with the vicissitudes of life and reaping the harvest of our reawakening. Metaphorically speaking, we might say that our good and wise conduct will retransform the wilted blossom of our present existence into that exquisite lotus flower, majestically "growing in mud and bowing to life as it is."

CONCLUSION

A Secular Encyclical has proposed to explore a simple problem: the grave social and moral crisis in which our present-day society and the environment we call "the world" are mired. Simple problems frequently have simple solutions, but simple solutions are, alas, often anything but simple to identify. That is because, in the philosophical forest, we cannot always see the ontological woods for the trees.

When we turn our attention to eliminating the very serious crisis in which both we as thinkers and our world as environment are entrapped, we find that it is we ourselves as human beings who have played a major role in creating that unsettling crisis and we, too, who play a lamentable part in failing to solve the resulting dilemma. More than that, however, our discussion confronts the extent to which we are remiss in not using completely or even adequately the inherent qualities and capabilities of our nature to manage wisely and effectively our lives and our environment. For one thing, we have persisted in clinging to obsolete beliefs, born of our primeval ignorance. Our blind and callow adherence to those unworthy thought patterns is surely one of the principal reasons for our failure to understand our own nature or to interact well both with others and with the world we share with others.

Another aspect of our inability to develop the innate qualities necessary for social integration is the fact that we have never found a proper and fulsome way to harmonize our goals and needs with those of fellow humans. We regard "the other" as a competitor rather than as a teammate or partner, as a threat, a competitor and barrier rather than as an opportunity to grow and enrich ourselves beyond the limits of the self. As a result, the trait we instinctively use when we liaise with "otherness" is aggressiveness and hostility. Under that burden, our actions and our ability to integrate the self and the other have little hope of success.

According to *A Secular Encyclical*, the same is true of our relationships with institutions and governmental structures and the partnering role they could play with individuals in a common plan to build a good society. This interrelationship has done little to further that shared mission and as such is a further proof and symptom of our inability to create forward-moving and harmony-driven schemes of action.

The encyclical as presented here is secular in nature and by definition. By that we mean that its scope and its message as a guide are rooted in the hic et nunc ("here and now")—in the temporal, worldly and human dimension of reality rather than in the timeless, non-worldly and non-human order of existence that has always been championed by religion and spirituality. Being a secular encyclical does not suggest that, as such, this manifesto is at odds with what we traditionally label "spiritual" or "supernatural." Nevertheless, it does intimate that its center of gravity and moral thrust lie elsewhere. It also suggests that we are able to realize our true potential and possess more completely our true human nature by fully developing our qualities and the richness inherent in our human nature. A divine or supernatural presence need not necessarily be excluded from the human equation here. However, by the same token, it does not oblige us to grant it a defining or essential role in our self-realization.

READERS GUIDE

1. What prompted you to read this book?

2. What were your initial impressions, and did they change as you continued to read the book?

3. What did you expect of the book? Were your expectations fulfilled? Was it a "good read"?

4. Does the title of the book have any particular significance for you?

5. What do you think is the major theme of the book?

6. Is there any particular message, warning, or counsel for the reader? What is it?

7. How important is the subject of the book to you? How does it apply in your life?

8. Does the book accurately describe the current situation of individuals and our society?

9. What did you think about this subject before reading this book?

10. Did you learn anything new about the subject matter of the book?

11. Do you think that the issues discussed in the book are of great significance to enough people? Do you think there needs to be greater efforts made to educate people about these issues?

12. Did you find anything surprising in the book? What?

13. Did the book add to your knowledge or motivate you to read further about the subject?

14. Did you find the book thought-provoking? Did the book change your opinion about anything? What?

15. Did the book evoke any particular feelings about the subject matter and the issues involved?

16. If there were one thing in the book that you would improve, what would it be?

17. What do you think was the author's prime intention in writing this book?

18. Do you think the author's writing style is easy to read or difficult? How do you think it might be improved?

19. How relevant or relatable is the major theme and messages or counsel of the book to your own life or society?

20. Do you think that this book will change anyone's perspective or opinion on the subject?

21. Would you recommend this book to others? To whom? Why?

22. How meaningful, in general, was this book for you?

www.ingramcontent.com/pod-product-compliance
Lightning Source LLC
Chambersburg PA
CBHW010729270326
41930CB00018B/3421